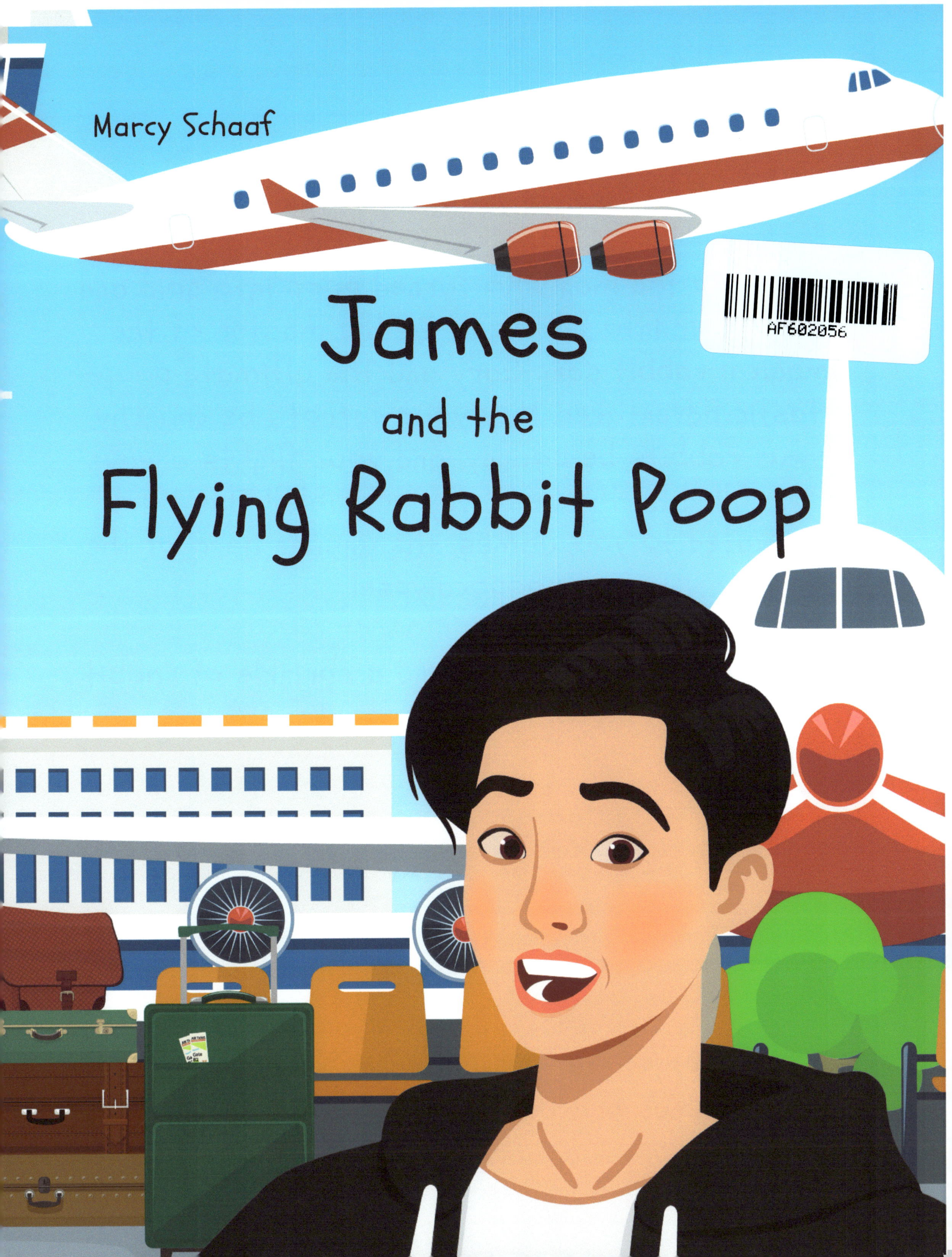
Marcy Schaaf
James
and the
Flying Rabbit Poop
AF602056

Dedicated to James Le

Here's to the man who turned poop into gold and laughter into fertilizer! To the master of the magical rabbit sanctuary and the ultimate poop-tastic adventurer. May your carrots be crunchy, your rabbits be bouncy, and your flights always poop-filled (in the best way possible)! This book is dedicated to you, James, the unsung hero of the poopocalypse!

With heaps of gratitude and a sprinkle of rabbit magic,

Introduction

Welcome to the whimsical world of James and the Flying Rabbit Poop! Get ready to embark on a journey filled with laughter, friendship, and a whole lot of poop! In this delightful tale, you'll meet James, a kind-hearted man with a passion for animals and a knack for turning poop into magic. Join James as he travels between the islands of Hawaii, spreading joy, nourishing gardens, and feeding hungry rabbits along the way. But beware, this story isn't your average bedtime read - it's packed with personality, charm, and a whole heap of fun! So, grab your imagination and let's dive into the enchanting world of James and his poop-tastic adventure!

Once upon a time, in the sunny paradise of Oahu, there lived a man named James.

James wasn't your ordinary fellow.
Nope, he was a bonafide animal lover
with a heart as big as the ocean.

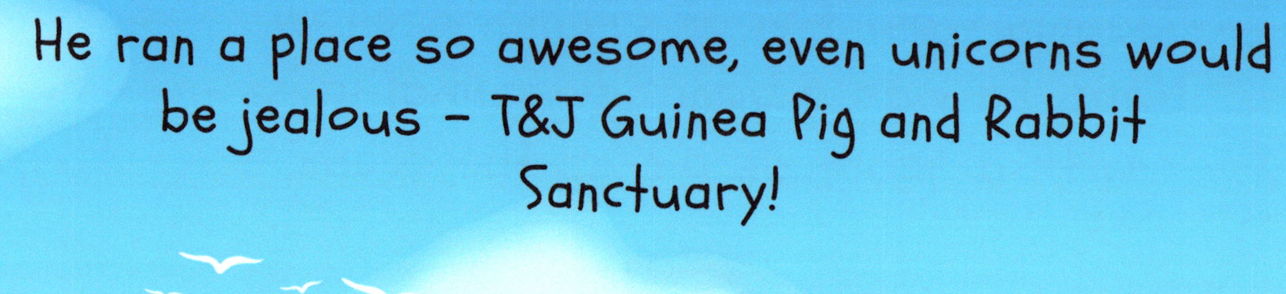

He ran a place so awesome, even unicorns would be jealous - T&J Guinea Pig and Rabbit Sanctuary!

Now, hold your horses, kiddos! What in the world is a sanctuary? Well, it's like a deluxe hotel for animals who need a little extra TLC.

At James's sanctuary, fluffy rabbits roamed free, doing bunny things like nibbling on carrots.

Once a week
James flies to the big island of
Hawaii.

HILO, HAWAII
But wait,
what's in his special delivery?
It's not clothes or toys,
it's... rabbit poop!

Now, don't go wrinkling your nose! This wasn't just any old poop. It was rabbit poop, and it was pure gold for a farmer on the big island!

This farmer was over the moon for James's poop. He'd sprinkle it on his garden like fairy dust, and bam! His veggies grew bigger than your wildest dreams!

Those veggies turned into scrumptious treats for the whole community.

Folks from all over the place would flock to the farmer's stand on Pakaka Rd, in Pahoa just to get a taste of his mouthwatering goodies.

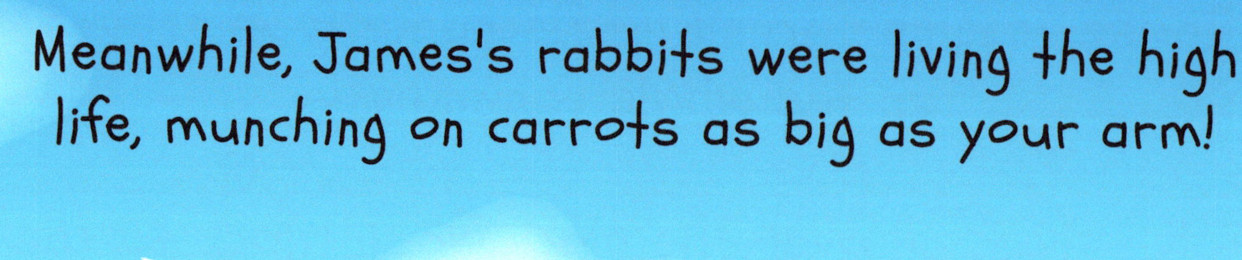

Meanwhile, James's rabbits were living the high life, munching on carrots as big as your arm!

It was like a never-ending circle of awesome! James brings poop, the farmer grows food, and the rabbits chow down.

And you know what they call this magical exchange? A barter system! It's like trading snacks with your pals - everybody wins!

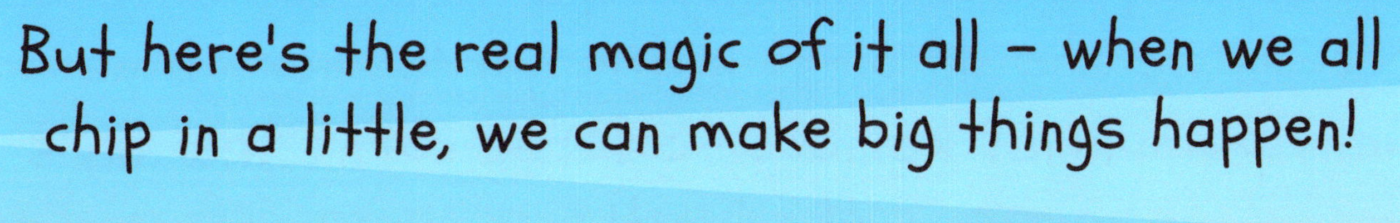

But here's the real magic of it all – when we all chip in a little, we can make big things happen!

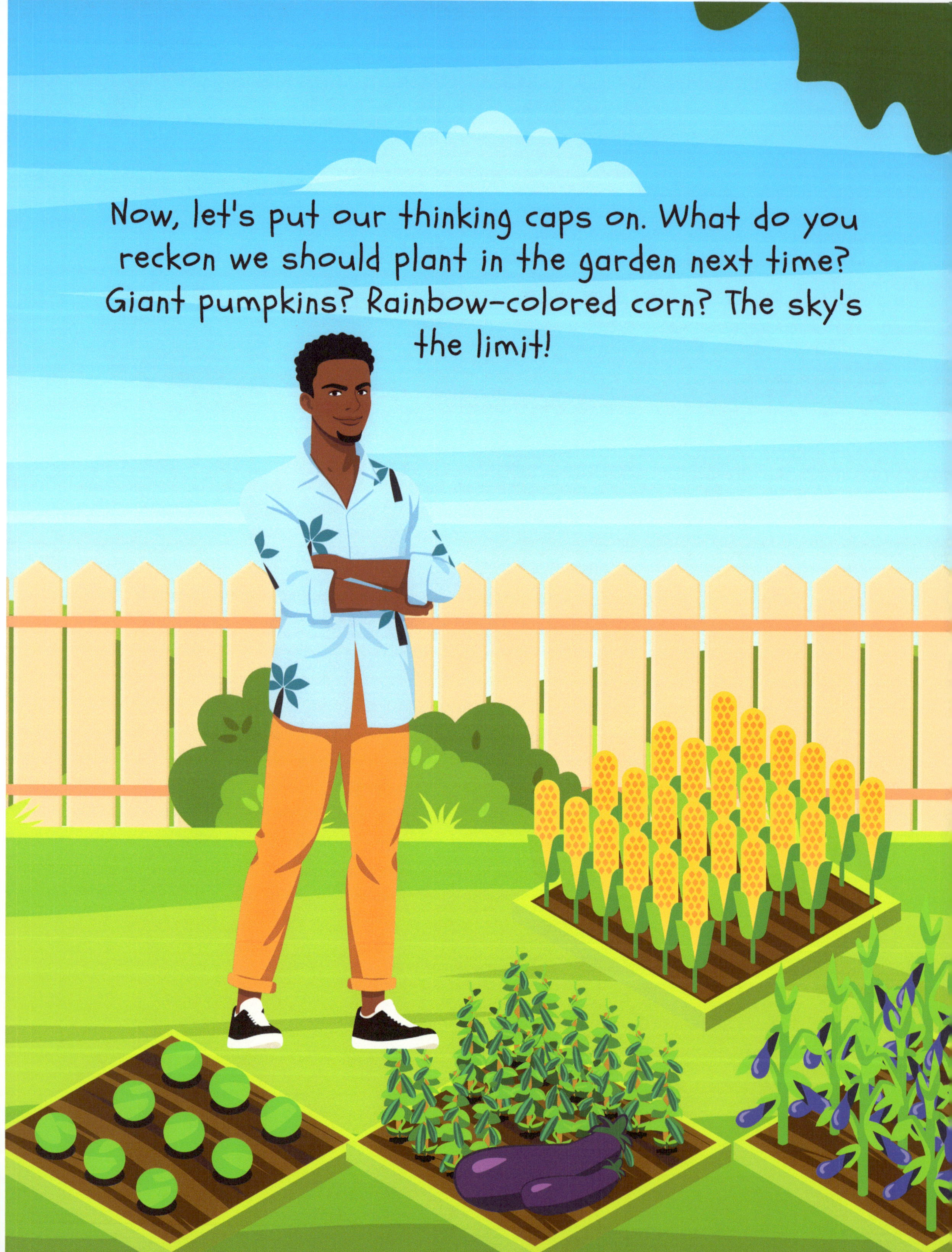
Now, let's put our thinking caps on. What do you reckon we should plant in the garden next time? Giant pumpkins? Rainbow-colored corn? The sky's the limit!

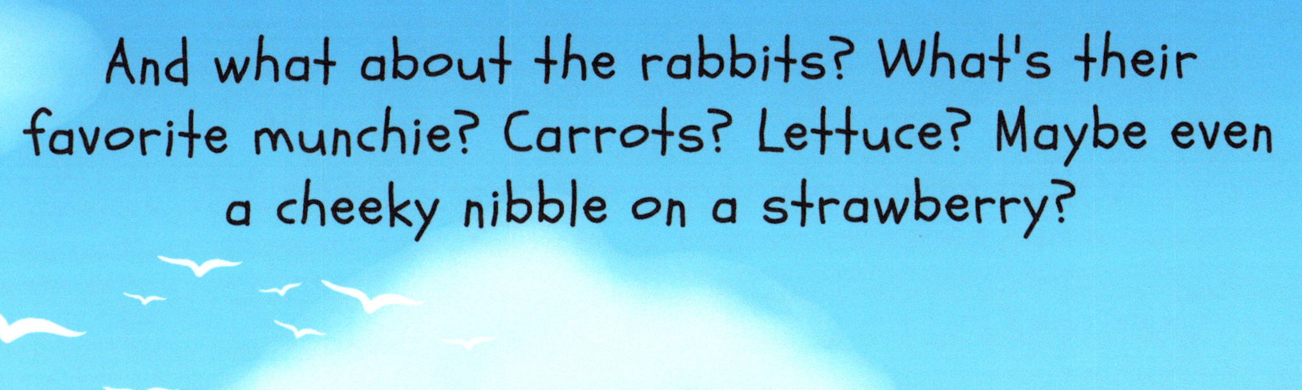

And what about the rabbits? What's their favorite munchie? Carrots? Lettuce? Maybe even a cheeky nibble on a strawberry?

Let's ask them! "Hey, bunnies, spill the beans! What's your ultimate snack attack?"

They twitch their whiskers and wiggle their tails – it seems they're fans of everything green and crunchy!

So, with James's rabbit poop, the farmer's garden, and the rabbits' insatiable appetites, the adventure rolls on!

But remember, it's not just about poop and food. It's about teamwork and spreading joy wherever you go!

When we all lend a hand, we can make the world a brighter, happier place for everyone!

So, the next time you see a garden bursting with life or a rabbit hopping with glee,

Think of James flying
with poop and remember
magic blooms from the
most unexpected places.

whether you're a rabbit, a farmer, or a poop-carrying superhero like James, there's always something you can do to make the world a better place!

And when we join forces and work together, there's no limit to the wonders we can achieve!

Now, let's buckle up and soar through the skies with James on one of his epic poop delivery missions!

Zoom! We're off, flying high above the clouds, headed straight for the big island of Hawaii!

Touchdown! We land at the Hilo airport, where the farmer eagerly awaits his special delivery.

James pops open his luggage, filled to the brim with bags of poop. The farmer's eyes light up like fireworks on the Fourth of July!

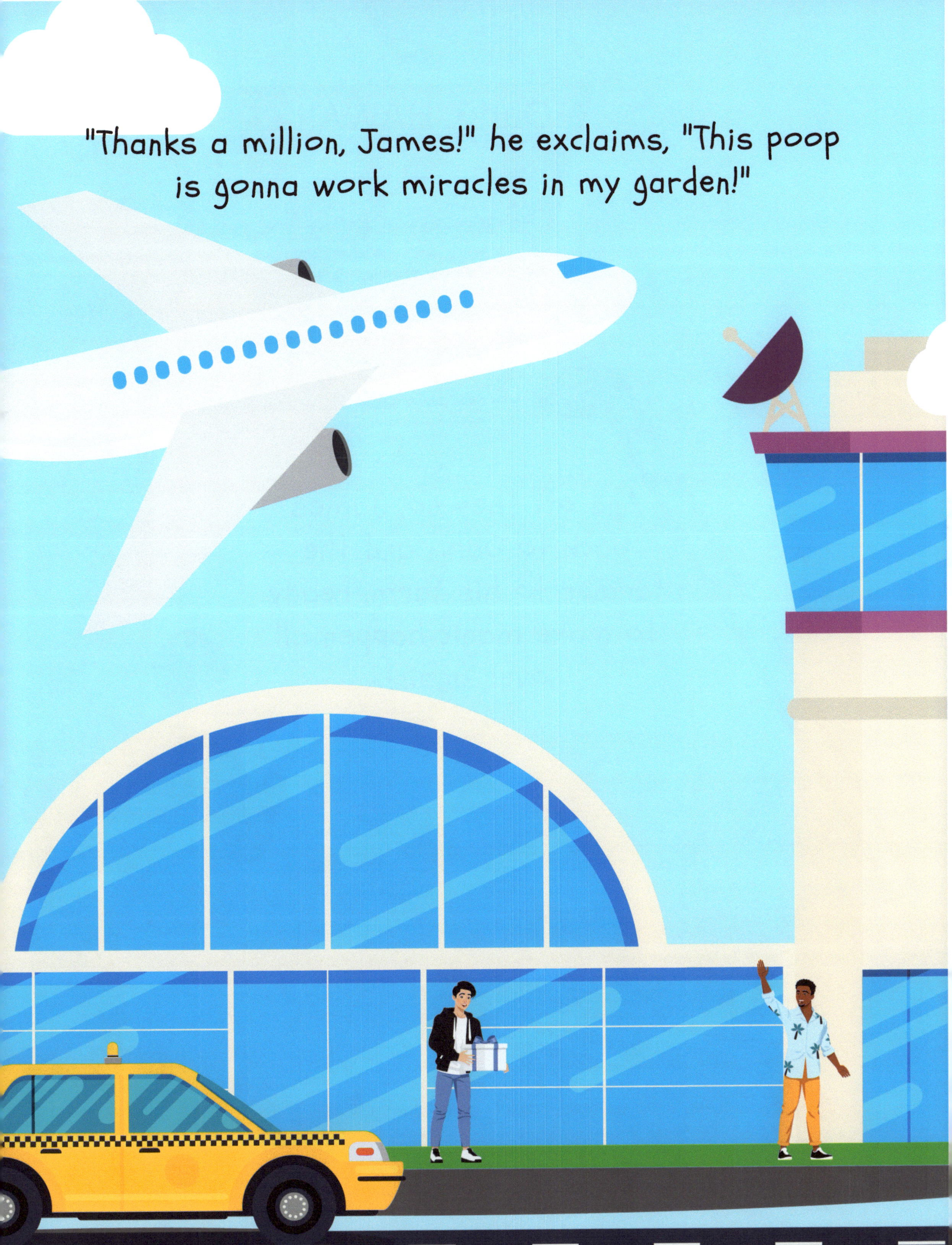
"Thanks a million, James!" he exclaims, "This poop is gonna work miracles in my garden!"

And off they go, James back to Oahu and the farmer to his farm, ready to make magic happen all over again!

Oahu, HAWAII
So, let's spread kindness like confetti and make the world a better place, one poop-filled adventure at a time!

The end...

T&J Guinea Pig and Rabbit Sanctuary
Kapolei, Oahu in the
Hawaiian Islands

The real James Le with Author Marcy Schaaf

Pakaka Rd
Farm Stand
located in Pahoa,
Hawaii

Books By Schaaf

www.BookBySchaaf.com

Find us at: